LEARNING ABOUT YOSEMITE With Grandma

BY JODY BRADY

For my five grandchildren: Quinn, Jaxon, Beckham, Jameson and Emmy

Copyright 2022 by Bradypus Publishing

No part of this book may be reproduced by any manner without the written permission of the publisher, except in brief quotations used in articles or reviews. Photos purchased from Shutterstock

For information contact:
Bradypus Publishing, 371 Nevada Street #7811
Auburn, CA 95604

THE VALLEY

Grandma went to Yosemite many times. She wants the kids to love it as much as she does. This is what she taught them.

#1 - Yosemite National Park in California is a wonder of nature.

The entire park covers miles and miles of forest and granite rock walls, some twice the height of the Empire State Building. It also has one of the tallest waterfalls in the world.
Almost all the land is designated wilderness - nothing can be built there. This is a picture of the famous Yosemite Valley.

GETTING AROUND

There are plenty of signs and maps to help people find their way around, and buses to get them from place to place.

There are places to eat, hotel rooms, nature centers, art galleries, and hiking trails where you see animals in the wild.

HALF DOME

This is Yosemite's most famous site, a one-of-a-kind formation. Millions of years ago, the valley was filled with glaciers. All but the top 700 feet of this granite mountain was buried in ice.

It had a crack from top to bottom. When the glaciers moved slowly away, they carried away the front part. Wind and weather had rounded the top into a dome shape. Only 4/5 of the dome remained. It would sound funny to call it 4/5 dome - so they named it Half Dome.

HIKING

Grandma said they could go on hikes; there are plenty of trails. Some are tough, some an easy stroll. They're all beautiful.

Remember: wear sunscreen, a hat, comfortable clothes and take water to drink – maybe snacks. Relax, breathe in fresh air and enjoy the GREAT outdoors.!

🌲 BACK TO NATURE 🌲

There are quiet, flat places to hike through forests, and nature centers to explore. Imagine the natives living here.

Walk silently, like the natives walked - you'll see and hear more wildlife. Birds and animals will hide if they hear you. Listen to the birds, and count how many colors of wildflowers you see.

DEER

There's a lot of wildlife in the park. You will often see deer. Sometimes you see one hiding — sometimes they are in a herd enjoying hanging out in a meadow. How many do you see?

Remember — don't feed them; it's not good for them to eat human food.

NATIVES

Native Americans have lived in Yosemite for nearly 4,000 years. There were more than thirty villages in the valley. They were divided into two groups. The Grizzly Bear was the symbol of all the villages on one side of the river.

The Coyote was the symbol of all the villages on the other side of the river. Sounds like sports teams – don't they? They only married a person from the opposite side of the river.
The name Yosemite is from the native word "uzumate," which meant grizzly bear. Eventually, people living outside the valley called all the natives, the Yosemite.

WHAT'S FOR DINNER?

One of the main foods natives ate was Acorn Mush. After shelling acorns, they pounded the kernels into a fine yellow meal, in mortar holes. Holes formed over time and can still be found on boulders like these.

The ground meal had to go through many processes before cooking and eating with their fingers. They also ate many types of berries; some berries they made into Cider.

Bears love Acorns as well. Luckily, acorns fall right before the bears hibernate for the winter. They need lots of calories before sleeping for months, so they eat up to 20,000 calories every day - eleven pounds of acorns. Yikes! That's A LOT of acorns.!!

NEVADA FALLS

VERNAL FALLS

Nevada Falls is upstream from Vernal, so it flows down to it. Both waterfalls can be seen from far away.

TRAILS

There are two trails to the falls, The John Muir Trail, and the Mist Trail. The Mist Trail is usually wet and slippery during the spring and summer. It's a good idea to wear a rain parka.

It's also important to wear good hiking shoes, not flip flops that can trip you. No one is allowed in the water anywhere near these falls; strong, fast-moving water is too dangerous.

THE MERCED RIVER

Nevada and Vernal Falls are known as the Giant Staircase. The Merced River flows over them and down into Yosemite Valley where it winds around the valley floor.

You **can** get in the water here. The river flows through meadows and forest with wonderful views. It is a habitat for millions of birds and animals. In the summer it is fun to raft but remember – its melted snow – it's COLD.!

THE VALLEY AND THE MOUNTAINS

This map shows the low and high areas. The green section is the Central Valley which receives some of the water from the Merced, which it needs. The valley is flat with rich soil; much of the U. S's food is grown there, especially fruits and nuts.

The orange areas are higher elevation. The dark orange is the Sierra Nevada Mountains where Yosemite is located. The green, low areas also include San Francisco and the Bay Area.

BEARS

There are about 300 – 500 bears in Yosemite. They are Brown Bears, even though they often look black. They don't approach humans, but they do break into cars or tents, if they smell food. It's important to lock up anything that smells!

It's also important to drive slowly in the park - bears sometimes get hit by cars. We need to protect them. Grizzly Bears are already extinct in California. The only place you will see one is on the California flag.

MARIPOSA GROVE

This grove of trees contains about 500 mature Giant Sequoia Trees, perhaps the largest living things on Earth. The most famous is one named Grizzly Giant. It is believed to be 2,700 years old.

It's amazing to walk through the grove. Look how huge the pinecones can grow

CALIFORNIA TUNNEL TREE

It's fun to walk right through this tree. You don't even need to duck your head. This tunnel was carved in 1895. In those days you could drive a horse-drawn carriage through it.

These are Sequoias, not Redwoods; they are different and live in different areas. Sequoias are the biggest trees in the world: big and thick. They live inland in higher, dry elevations. Redwoods are the tallest and live near the coast; they like fog.

ABE - TEDDY AND JOHN

President Lincoln signed the Yosemite Land Grant, in 1864, which protected Mariposa Gove and Yosemite Valley. It was the first time the government protected land for people to enjoy. Twenty-six years later it became a National Park.

John Muir and President Teddy Roosevelt both loved nature and the outdoors. Muir brought Teddy to see Yosemite and convinced him the whole area should be protected.
Thanks to these men we have wonderful National Parks.

💙 SQUIRRELS

There are four types of squirrels in Yosemite. They are rodents, but they're cute rodents. John Muir's favorite was the Douglas Squirrel (or Cickaree) They're the smallest and have an orange belly and white eye ring. They squeak. It's adorable.

Muir would sit and watch them for hours and whistle songs to the little guys. He wrote page after page about them.

"He is, without exception, the wildest animal I ever saw - a fiery, sputtering little bolt of life..... the squirrel of squirrels, flashing from branch to branch of his favorite evergreens...."

A WALK IN THE PARK

Upper and Lower Yosemite Falls, plus a middle section, form the highest waterfall in North America. All the water comes from Yosemite Creek, formed up high, entirely by melted snow.

The walk to the base of the lower falls is an easy, flat stroll. In the spring if there has been a lot of rain and snow, the falls are full and you'll get sprayed with mist. It feels great.!

CLIMBING THE DOME

This hike is only for brave and in-shape hikers. It is an all day hike up and back. Some people camp overnight and take two days. The top is 8,844 feet above sea level.

When you get to the dome, there are big wire cables bolted into the rock. Hikers grab the cables on each side, wearing gloves hopefully and pull themselves up.
See how tiny the hikers look.

DON'T LOOK DOWN

This is what it looks like when there are A LOT of people climbing the dome. Grandma has climbed it three times (she had to brag – even though she tells the kids not to :)

This is someone climbing El Capitan. Grandma tells the kids not to rock climb because it would worry her too much. "If you do – don't tell me."

WILDLIFE

Keep your eyes open and walk on the less busy paths; you can see lots of wild animals. They're more afraid of you – than you are of them. Coyotes can be seen in the meadows looking for a snack, like a mouse or rabbit.

Grandma loves California King Snakes. She tells the kids, "Don't touch them and they won't bother you. They won't chase you down to bite you. Look how beautiful they are."

🌍 HEAVEN ON EARTH.!

The kids learned a lot about Yosemite. Grandma said they would go visit it real soon, maybe in the Fall or Winter when there are fewer people.
The quiet is awesome!

The kids agreed —
We all need to take care of nature
and our National Parks.

Printed in the USA
CPSIA information can be obtained
at www.ICGtesting.com
LVHW062227150424
777514LV00029B/170